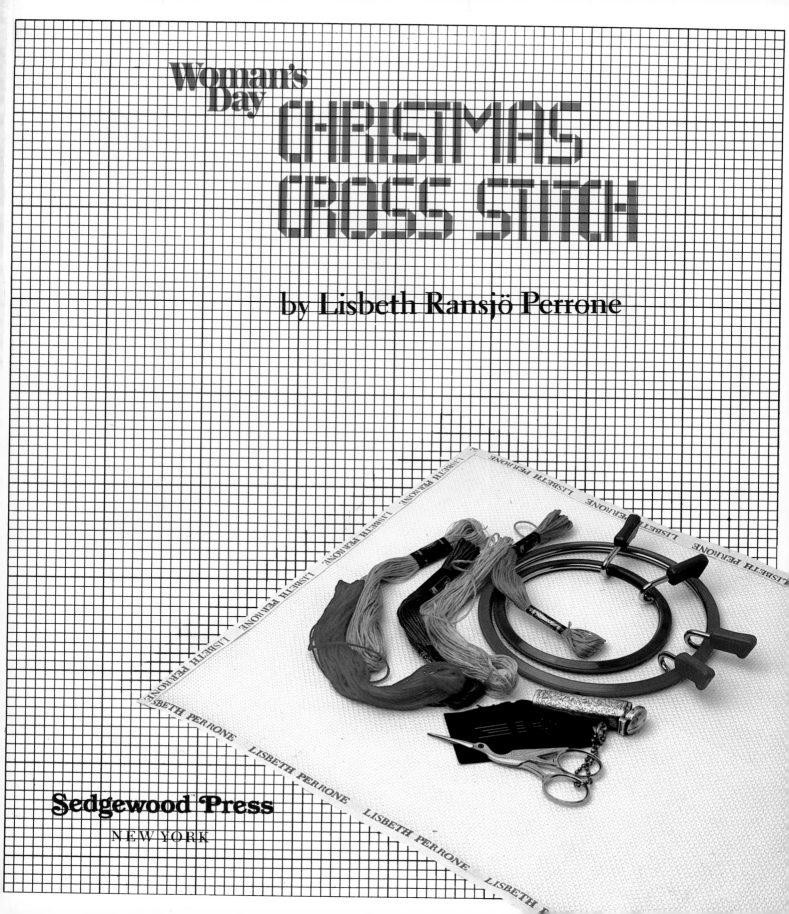

Woman's Day

CHRISTMAS CROSS STITCH

by Lisbeth Ransjö Perrone

Sedgewood Press

NEW YORK

For CBS Inc.

Editorial Director: *Dina von Zweck*
Project Coordinator: *Ruth Josimovich*

For Sedgewood Press™

Editorial Director, Sedgewood™ Press: *Jane Ross*
Project Director: *Elizabeth Rice*
Managing Editor: *Gale Kremer*
Designer: *Bentwood Studio/Jos. Trautwein*
Production Manager: *Bill Rose*

Photography

Robert H. Epstein

Distributed in the Trade by Van Nostrand Reinhold
ISBN 0-442-28188-9
Library of Congress Catalog Number 83-60328
Manufactured in the United States of America

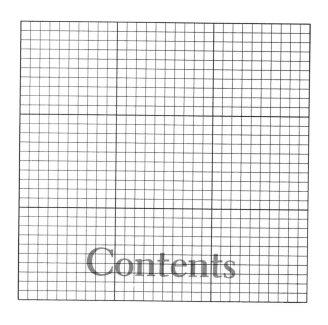

Contents

ACKNOWLEDGMENTS

I would like to extend my deep appreciation and thanks to some very talented and creative needle-artists: to my mother, Thomazine Ransjö, and to Yoke Abolafi van Berge Henegouwen and Nora Pickens for their help in embroidering the projects for the book; and to Mary Jo Hays and Sandy Erickson, whose skill and craftsmanship resulted in work-charts that are as meticulous as they are beautiful. Working with these very special people has truly been a joyous experience.

LISBETH RANSJÖ PERRONE

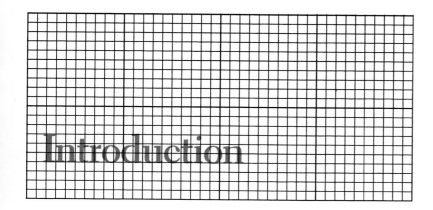

Introduction

Christmas enchants all people, adults and children alike. It is a time filled with anticipation, wonder and love, accompanied by cherished customs and traditions. These customs and traditions vary among families, regions and countries. Common to all, though, on this annual festival, is "Santa Claus." No matter what precise form this jovial figure takes, or by what name he is known, he symbolizes generosity, peace and kindness.

Christmastime is also universally a time for rejoicing, exchanging of presents and greetings, feasting happily together and festively decorating our trees and homes.

This book is about a particular form of decoration: Christmas needlework. The feeling in this work is a reflection of the season itself. What could be more appropriate than to decorate our homes with Christmas scenes and symbols done in beautiful cross stitch embroidery? And what could express better the joy of the season? Here are pieces that will become part of your own family Christmas traditions, brought out and enjoyed year after year. A piece of needlework also makes a very special and personal gift.

Woman's Day Christmas Cross Stitch is a workbook of some 50 Christmas designs. Do think of it as that: a workbook. You can use the designs and color combinations as shown; or you can feel free to change the colors, use different materials, rearrange the designs. Create your own designs from the scenes and figures provided. This book offers endless possibilities and hours of enjoyment now and in years to come. Enjoy the projects—and enjoy this season of warmth and sharing.

General Instructions

Each design in *Woman's Day Christmas Cross Stitch* is worked in cross stitch and shown in full color; each has its own work-chart.

The Work-Charts

Each work-chart is done in symbols. Each symbol represents one stitch, worked in a specific color. When a symbol changes on the chart, that means there is also a change in the color thread used. Each chart has a color-key for the symbols; the actual color is given, and a number as well. The number corresponds to the exact color of DMC cotton embroidery floss that was used for the project pictured. (If you can't find the precise color specified, simply use one that's similar—because the color range is so wide, a number close to the one we used will be fine.)

The grid of the chart represents your material. (The material is integral to the project, in that it is the background of your finished piece.) Each square on the grid represents the area for one stitch. Blank squares in the charts stand for areas left unstitched. If a chart extends over more than one page it shows clearly how and where to continue on to the next work-chart.

When you work on any of the projects in this book, *always* follow the chart. Because the projects were done mostly freehand, the chart has, in some cases, been modified slightly, so that chart and photograph may not be exactly alike. In most cases, they are—but when there is a difference, it is the chart you should follow.

Note that letters for the Christmas stockings are not charted (you'll choose your own letters—see page 137), so the charts for the stockings are shorter.

Except for the small Christmas ornaments, all charts are centered vertically and horizontally. This makes both counting stitches and centering your material easier.

Mirror-Images

A few of the charts have been shown as half motifs. These have to be "mirror-imaged." This means that you simply reverse the chart from the center. If you find this hard to do, or confusing, here's a tip. I tell my students and readers to rechart the design as shown in the book on regular graph paper, using felt-tip coloring pens. The ink from the felt-tips is absorbed through the paper. When the half of the design given in the book is charted, turn your graph paper over: there is your mirror-image.

Cross Stitch

To make any of the designs shown in the book you need to know only two embroidery stitches: the cross stitch and the backstitch.

The cross stitch is a stitch of symmetry and coordination. Together, these stitches become lovely forms and shapes. The stitch has a long history; over the years, folk tales were perpetuated through woven and cross-stitched textiles.

This time-honored embroidery technique is very popular these days—and with reason. It is very easy to do. Less expensive and time-consuming than many other types of embroidery, cross stitch has many functional as well as decorative applications. A completed cross stitch is composed of two diagonal stitches, which form an "x." The crosses should be of an even shape and size. You can work this stitch horizontally or vertically. Work cross stitch from left to right, or top to bottom, forming half the cross each time; then come back and cross over to complete your stitches. The top stitches should always slant in the same direction.

Cross stitch is always worked on an even-weave or even-weave squared fabric. (You must be able to count the threads or squares in the material.) When worked on an even-weave material, the x is done over two threads in each direction. On an even-weave squared fabric, the x is stitched over one square of the material. (See Diagrams A and B.)

Backstitch

Backstitching is used to highlight or outline a figure or shape. It is also used for connecting these figures and shapes. It can be worked diagonally, vertically, or horizontally over two threads (for even-weaves) or over one square (for even-weave squared material). Backstitches should be worked from right to left (see Diagram C). Note that a backstitch is shown as a straight line on the charts in this book.

Tools and Materials

Using the appropriate tools and materials will make all the difference in your work. Take the time to get exactly what you need, and you'll be amply rewarded. If you're unsure of what to buy, ask at a nearby needlework shop. You'll usually find someone there who'll be happy to advise you.

Embroidery Basket or Other Storage Unit

Keep all your materials and tools gathered together in one place. They should be easily accessible and portable. If they're not, you are likely to lose that "spur of the moment" desire to create and stitch a particular design.

DIAGRAM A

Cross stitch done on even-weave linen

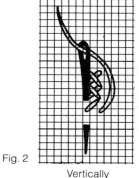

Horizontally   Fig. 1

Fig. 2

Vertically

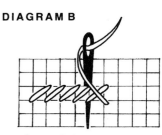

DIAGRAM B

Cross stitch done on even-weave squared fabric

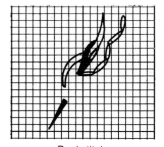

DIAGRAM C

Backstitch

7

Needles

Needles used for cross stitch embroidery should have a blunt end. Sizes 24 and 26 are suitable unless you use a coarse material and coarse thread.

Scissors

A pair of sharp embroidery scissors is a must. I have found that a pair of old-fashioned "stork scissors" takes care of all needs for cross stitch.

Thimble

If you are used to working with a thimble, you'll find that one that is deep and rounded will serve you best.

Markers

There are some wonderful water-soluble markers available. They are great for indicating outlines or guidelines. If necessary, you can eliminate these lines from finished work with a wet sponge or dampened towel. (Felt-tip coloring pens are excellent if you plan to rechart for mirror-images—see page 6. Note that these are not water soluble; use them on graph paper only.)

Push Pins

It is always useful to have a box of rustproof push pins in your storage unit. You may need them for blocking or stretching, or to hang up a partially worked design so that you can study it.

Embroidery Hoop or Frame

Personally, I never use a frame or hoop for cross stitch embroidery because the cross stitch technique does not force or pull the material out of shape. However, if you are used to working with a frame or hoop, I recommend a light one.

Notebook

Ideas and creations feed each other. You'll forget ideas if you don't write them down as they occur.

Even-Weave Materials

Cross stitch, as we have mentioned, is always done on an even-weave or even-weave squared material. (Unless a particular project specifies otherwise, we have used a #19 even-weave linen throughout the book.)

Even-weaves come in different widths, coarsenesses and colors. The lower the number the coarser the material. The coarseness, or fineness, is measured by the number of stitches per inch. However, there is a difference between *even-weave linens* and *even-weave squared fabrics*.

On even-weave linens the cross stitch covers two threads in each direction. This means that on a #19 even-weave material you will get 9.5 stitches per inch. An even-weave squared material is measured by the number of squares per inch. The cross stitch covers one square of the material. A #19 even-weave squared fabric would therefore give you 19 stitches per inch. It is important to know this difference, because—as you can see—it makes a difference of 100% in the size.

Until you become really familiar with the different even-weave materials on the market, consult with people at your local needlework shop as to what size and type of material would be best for a certain project. Most of the needlework stores throughout the country now stock an assortment of even-weave materials. The most common even-weave squared fabrics are Aida and Hardanger cotton cloths.

Threads

A good rule to remember when you pick a thread for your even-weaves is to choose one that is equal in coarseness or fineness to the warp and weft thread in the material. This combination will give a nice fullness to your embroidery. There should be no struggle, or weakness, in this combination. The thread should flow easily in and out of the material and give your stitches good coverage. By this I mean that there should be no tension between thread and material; rather, there should be harmony and balance between the two. If the material pulls, the thread is too heavy for it; if the thread is too thin, you'll get inadequate coverage.

When you use a metallic silver or gold thread, follow the same principle. Choose a thread that is compatible with the material, so that it will glide easily through the even weave. Don't pick a metallic thread with a cotton center strand—it will ravel as you work with it.

Throughout this book we have used 6-strand DMC cotton embroidery floss. The advantage of this thread is that the strands can be easily separated, as well as added to; therefore, it's suitable for most even-weave materials. It is also easily obtainable throughout this country and other countries. Of course, you can use any thread you like as long as it's suitable for cross stitch. We used 4 strands of 6-strand DMC thread for our #19 even-weave linens.

How To Start a Project and Follow a Chart

Once you have selected a design it is time to obtain your background material and threads. Remember that the best quality will give the best result. Do not compromise when it comes to quality.

We have included specific information about both material and thread for each project. Again, consult with a needlework shop if you wish to change the size, work with a different mesh, or otherwise adapt the project.

Allow enough material for mounting and finishing your piece. Unlike needlepoint canvas, which is filled entirely with stitches, the background material for cross stitch embroidery is an integral part of the finished design.

Prepare your fabric by whipstitching around the edges with a regular sewing thread. (To whipstitch, insert a threaded sewing needle at a right angle to the fabric edge. Make overcast stitches over the edge, spacing them evenly, at a uniform depth. The resulting slanted stitches will keep the edges from fraying.)

Find the center of your material by folding it lightly in half: first horizontally, then vertically. Where the two folds intersect baste a temporary guideline in a contrasting color. Find the center of your work-chart. Start your work from the center. I always do, because doing so gives me a sense of proportion as well as allowing for possible changes or additions around the edges.

Follow the chart carefully. You will soon find that your eyes adjust automatically to counting stitches, both in the material you're working with and on the work-chart. Your eye will pick up an error quickly. (Work in a good light—not only for cross stitch, but for doing any kind of embroidery.)

The thread you are working with should not be longer than 18 inches. Don't knot your thread. Securely fasten the beginning and end of each thread by weaving it in and out on the back of existing stitches on your work. Fasten the thread in the direction of the stitches. Do not carry your thread on the back from one area to another; it is likely to show through if you do.

How To Finish Your Cross-Stitched Work

When the actual "stitching" is done, a few more steps are required to complete your work: checking; cleaning; blocking (if needed); mounting.

Checking

Check your work carefully. Hold it up to the light. Any stitches that have been left out will be obvious through the light. If you have forgotten any, fill them in.

Make sure that all ends are securely fastened on the back. Trim unnecessarily long threads on the back.

Cleaning

If your work needs cleaning, wash it in lukewarm water with a very mild soap solution. Rinse in cold water. Do not wring out. Place the wet work on a terrycloth towel; roll it up gently while pressing the water out. While it is still moist, press your work face down and then let it dry thoroughly.

Blocking

This step usually isn't needed with cross stitch embroidery, because this technique doesn't pull the material out of shape. If you feel it is needed for a particular piece, first make a blocking board from a piece of insulating wallboard. (Make sure that pins can be easily pushed into it.) Glue or staple graph paper to the board, then wrap it with a thin clear plastic sheet. Now squeeze a mild soap solution through a clean sponge and run it lightly over the back of your piece until the material is well dampened. Go easy—don't press or rub. Lay the material (face up) on the blocking board. Fasten your piece (at quarter-inch intervals) with rustproof push pins or tacks, using the graph paper as a guide. Remove the material when it has dried completely. If the piece is still slightly out of shape, repeat the procedure.

Mounting

For mounting your work yourself, consult one of the many good books that are available on the subject.

If you're framing your piece, make sure that it is mounted on an acid-free rag or museum board. Use a light-surfaced backing if your embroidery is done on a light-colored material, and a dark-surfaced backing if it was done on a dark material.

Most needlework stores also carry a variety of ready-made products like trays, ornaments, footstools, frames and so on that are very easy to assemble.

Jolly Christmas Stocking

With a hearty "HO HO HO," this stocking proclaims a message of sheer good spirits. Adorned with packages and candy canes, a poinsettia and holly, and smiling gingerbread men, it gives a hint of the treasures to be found within.

If you want to include the message at the top, or a name, allow extra material (you can use the Cross Stitch Alphabet on page 137 for the appropriate letters).

As pictured: Cut size—20 x 14". Finished size—16" long; 8" wide at top. (These dimensions include enough material for the letters at the top.) #19 even-weave linen; 4 strands of thread.

O =   Green 700—1 skein

L =   Brown 938—2 skeins

W =   White—1 skein

X =   Red 666—1 skein

/ =   Dark Green 895—1 skein

Y =   Yellow 307—1 skein

+ =   Dark Red 816—1 skein

V =   Maroon 814—1 skein

◢ =   Lavender 718—1 skein

● =   Purple 553—1 skein

‰ =   Turquoise 996—1 skein

14

15

"Peace on Earth" Pillow

This project, with its simple and direct message, would make an attractive wall hanging as well as a pillow. Appropriate at any time of year, it is especially meaningful as an expression of the spirit of the Christmas season. It is an easy project, sure to be appreciated by all, with its circle of loving doves. The birds are outlined in a dark grey backstitch.

As pictured: Cut size—17 x 17". Finished size—13 x 13".
#19 even-weave linen; 4 strands of thread.

X = Red 666–1 skein

❦ = Blue 797–1 skein

/ = Dark Green 986–2 skeins

+ = Light Green 905–2 skeins

◢ = Dark Grey 413–2 skeins

V = Light Grey 762–2 skeins

Musical Elves

This is another version of our cover project. Full of Christmas spirit, these little imps really do look as if they're making a "joyful noise," don't they? The backstitches in the elves' faces are done in red. The drumsticks are done in brown backstitches. (See the Cross Stitch Numbers on page 137; use it as your guide if you wish to change the date.)

X = Red 666–2 skeins

/ = Dark Green 987–2 skeins

+ = Light Green 989–1 skein

V = Dark Gold 781–1 skein

● = Gold 783–2 skeins

‰ = Blue 813–1 skein

L = Flesh 758–1 skein

As pictured: Cut size — 24¼ x 21¾″. Finished size — 20¼ x 17¾″.
#19 even-weave linen; 4 strands of thread.

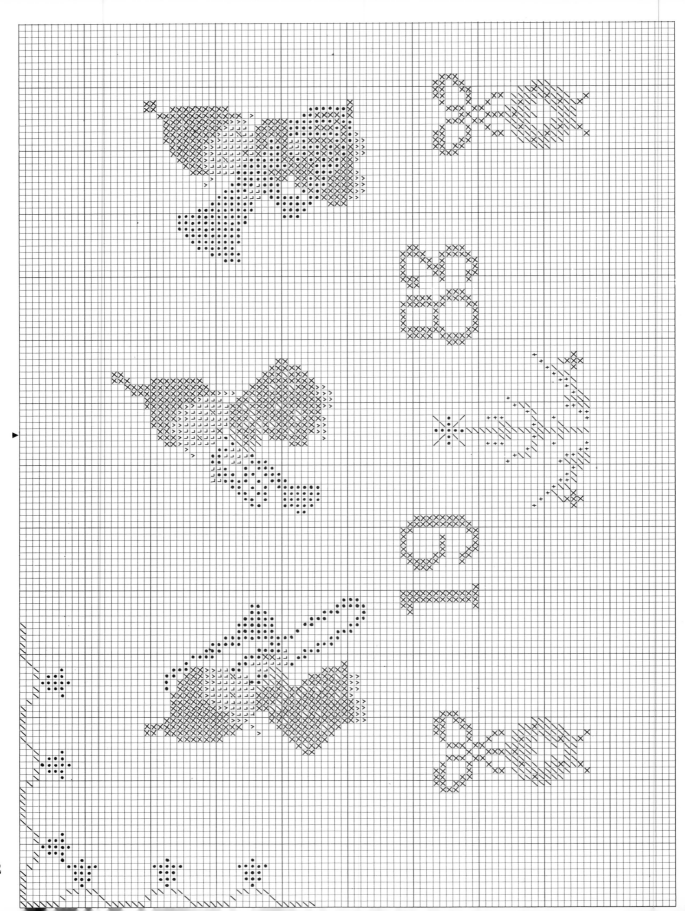

23

The Three Wise Men

The three kings, riding their camels to Bethlehem, form a simple and peaceful evening scene. This striking project, suitable for "cross stitchers" of every skill level, is worked in blue and grey. The moon is outlined with backstitches done in a metallic silver thread.

As pictured: Cut size — 15½ x 19½". Finished size — 11½ x 15½".
#19 even-weave linen; 4 strands of thread.

❅ = Blue 797–3 skeins

+ = Grey 928–2 skeins

Metallic Silver Thread–4 yards

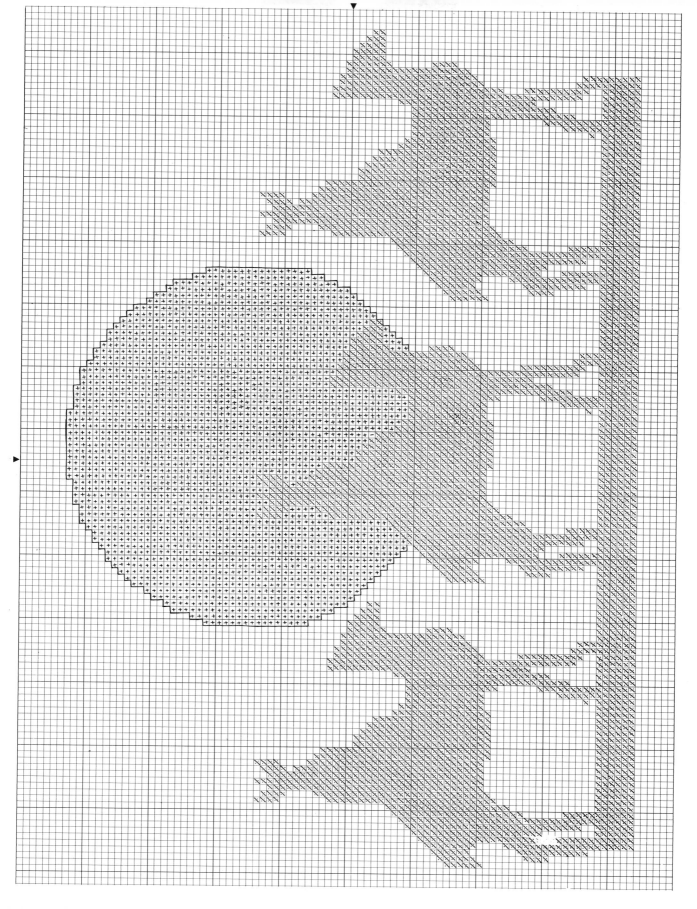

Partridge in a Pear Tree

The feeling of exhilaration in this project will make you want to sing along with its cheerful message. This is whimsical and a lot of fun, with its variety of colors—and it's easy to do.

As pictured: Cut size — 19¾ x 15⅝". Finished size — 15¾ x 11⅝".
#19 even-weave linen; 4 strands of thread.

/ =   Dark Green 3345–1 skein

O =   Green 700–1 skein

+ =   Light Green 703–1 skein

Y =   Yellow 727–1 skein

V =   Brown 898–1 skein

L =   Dark Beige 840–1 skein

▼ =   Dark Grey 317–1 skein

● =   Turquoise 996–1 skein

‰ =   Blue 820–1 skein

X =   Red 666–1 skein

◢ =   Pink 3354–1 skein

31

"Pairs of Ladies" Runner

This is a dramatic but very simple repeat pattern. It's versatile, too—you can work it in different colors, make it as long or short as you like. This particular motif is quite effective as a border or tablecloth center, too.

As pictured: Cut size—26½ x 14". Finished size—22½ x 10".
#19 even-weave linen; 4 strands of thread.

Y =   Yellow 444—1 skein

/ =   Dark Red 816—2 skeins

X =   Medium Red 321—2 skeins

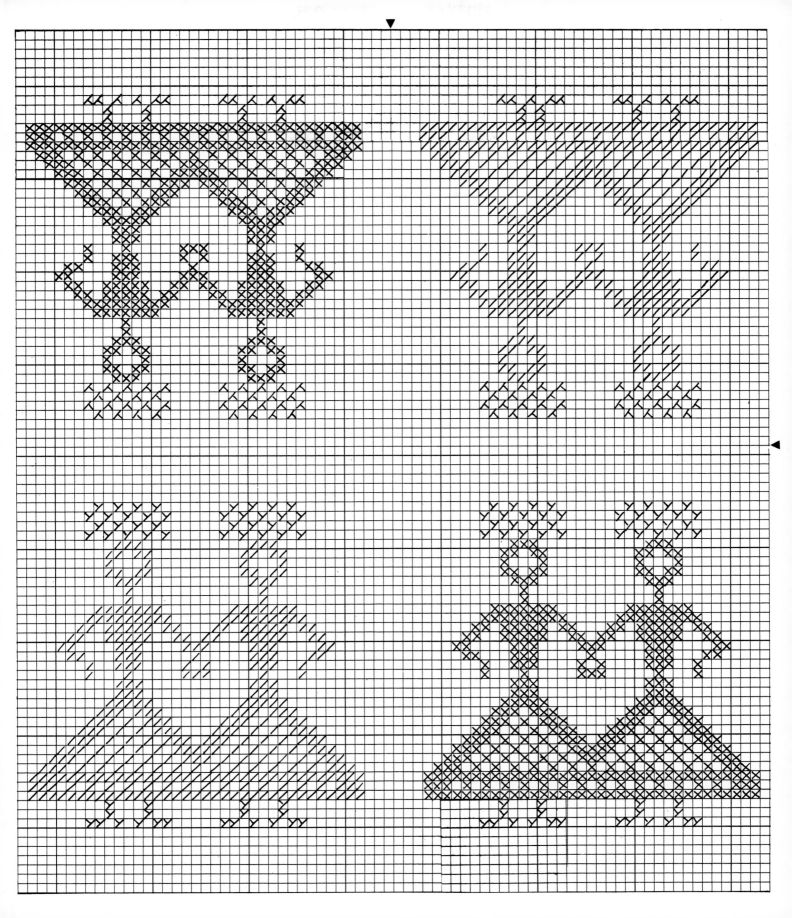

"Jump For Joy" Pillow

Our rotund little pig expresses perfectly the exuberant sentiments of the season. "What fun! My favorite time of year—here at last!" he seems to say. His mouth is outlined in a dark grey backstitch.

As pictured: Cut size — 10½ x 12½". Finished size — 6½ x 8½".
#19 even-weave linen; 4 strands of thread.

X =   Red 666–1 skein

♣ =   Light Blue 813–2 skeins

O =   Green 700–1 skein

● =   Pink 3354–1 skein

+ =   Grey 318–1 skein

Angel Orchestra

What would Christmas be without angels? This heavenly choir creates a feeling of instant harmony, emphasizing the joy of the season.

If you prefer, replace the heart with your initials (see the Cross Stitch Alphabet on page 137). There are backstitches in medium brown inside the harps. For most of the angels, the bottoms of the skirts are backstitched in red.

X =	Red 666–3 skeins
/ =	Dark Green 937–3 skeins
● =	Gold 782–2 skeins
V =	Medium Brown 434–1 skein
L =	Flesh 758–1 skein
+ =	Medium Pink 3326–1 skein
‰ =	Light Blue 827–1 skein
■ =	Metallic Silver Thread–4 yards

As pictured: Cut size—24 x 21¼". Finished size—20 x 17¼".
#19 even-weave linen; 4 strands of thread.

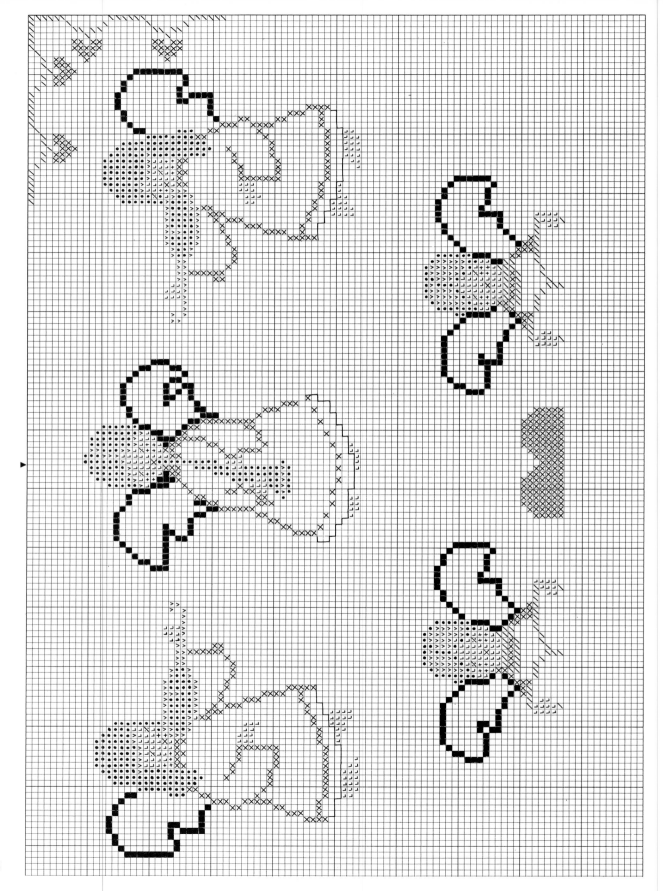

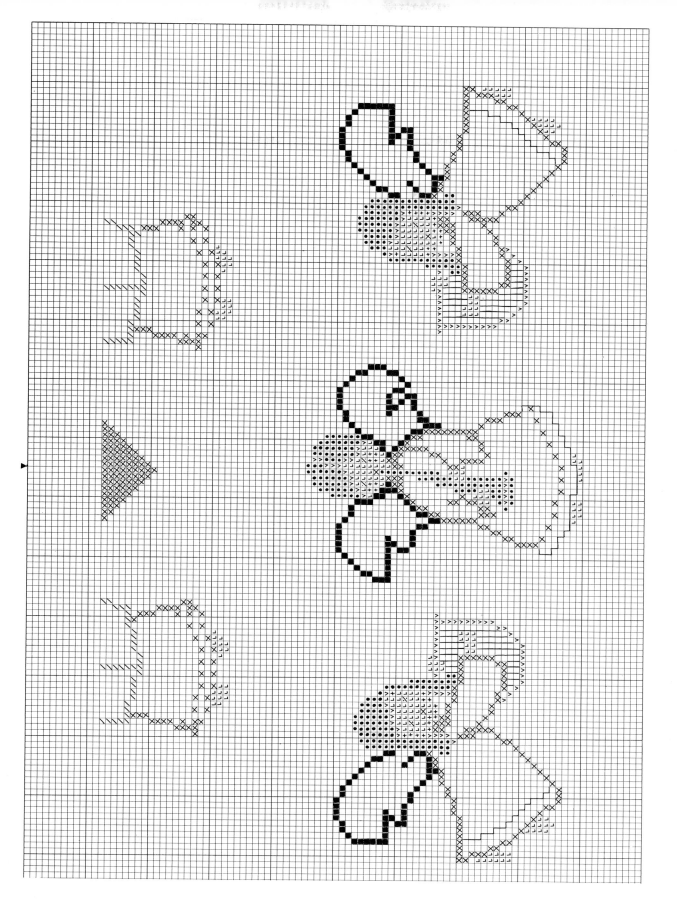

Geometric Christmas Tree

This is a contemporary and highly stylized project that will effectively "spruce up" your home and complement other holiday decorations. It's easy and quick, and creates the instant drama of a wintry night with its golden stars and dark-to-light shades of green.

As pictured: Cut size—17½ x 16″. Finished size—13½ x 12″.
#19 even-weave linen; 4 strands of thread.

/ =   Dark Green 937–2 skeins

O =   Green 700–2 skeins

+ =   Light Green 907–2 skeins

■ =   Metallic Gold Thread–4 yards

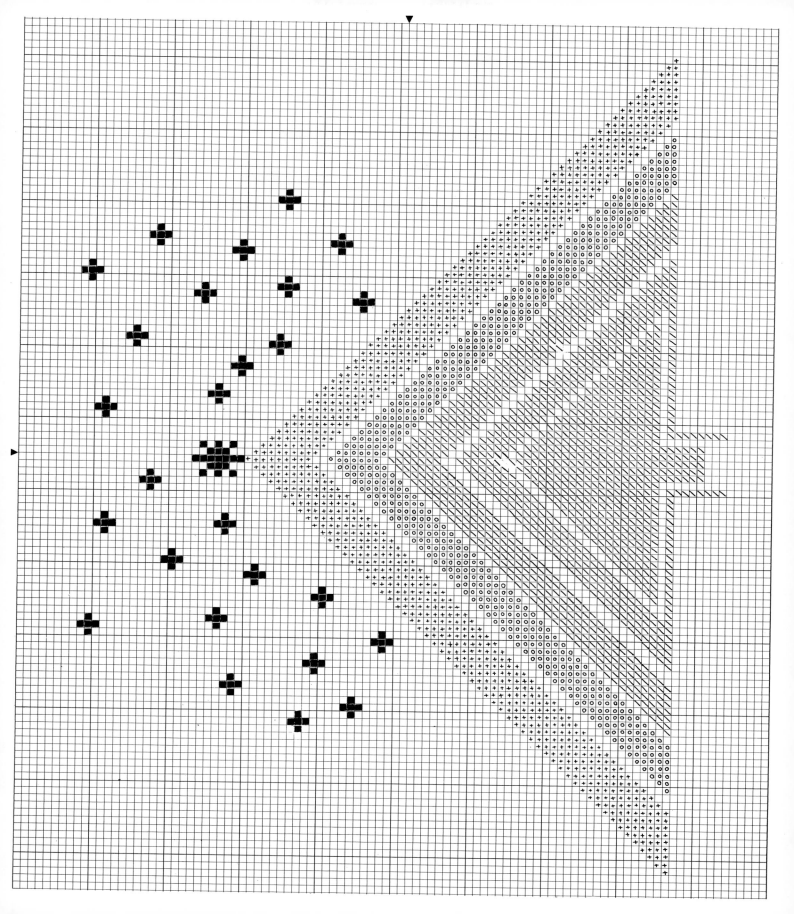

Reindeer and Elves Christmas Stocking

These bustling, mischievous little elves are busy filling the stocking with exciting surprises. (The reindeer pulling the sleigh looks a bit apprehensive—have Santa's little helpers been playing tricks on him again?)

This colorful project has a lot going on, and is sure to thrill a youngster. Allow extra material on top if you plan to personalize it with a child's name. Use the Cross Stitch Alphabet on page 137 for the name (include the branches, too, if you like). The back-stitches in the faces of the elves are done in dark grey.

As pictured: Cut size—20 x 14". Finished size—16" long; 8" wide at top. (These dimensions include enough material for a name at the top.) #19 even-weave linen; 4 strands of thread.

X =	Red 666—1 skein
/ =	Dark Green 895—1 skein
+ =	Light Green 704—1 skein
Y =	Yellow 973—1 skein
C =	Turquoise 996—1 skein
% =	Blue 797—1 skein
● =	Pink 956—1 skein
◢ =	Burgundy 902—1 skein
O =	Green 700—1 skein
B =	Black—1 skein
W =	White—1 skein
T =	Light Orange 972—1 skein
L =	Flesh 951—1 skein
V =	Dark Gold 781—1 skein
△ =	Dark Beige 840—1 skein
▼ =	Dark Grey 317—1 skein

51

Christmas Bells Tablecloth

A cheerful way to dress up a holiday table, this festive tablecloth and napkin set would be appropriate for a casual or a formal get-together. It's a simple, mirror-imaged design (see page 6 for tips on working mirror-images). We cross stitched a leaf from the center design (of the tablecloth) in the corner of the napkin.

As pictured: Cut size—60 x 48". Finished size—56 x 44".
(Napkins: Cut size—15½ x 15½". Finished size—11½ x 11½".)
#19 even-weave linen; 4 strands of thread.

53

O = Green 700–2 skeins

+ = Light Green 966–2 skeins

Y = Light Orange 972–2 skeins

W = White–2 skeins

V = Dark Gold 781–1 skein

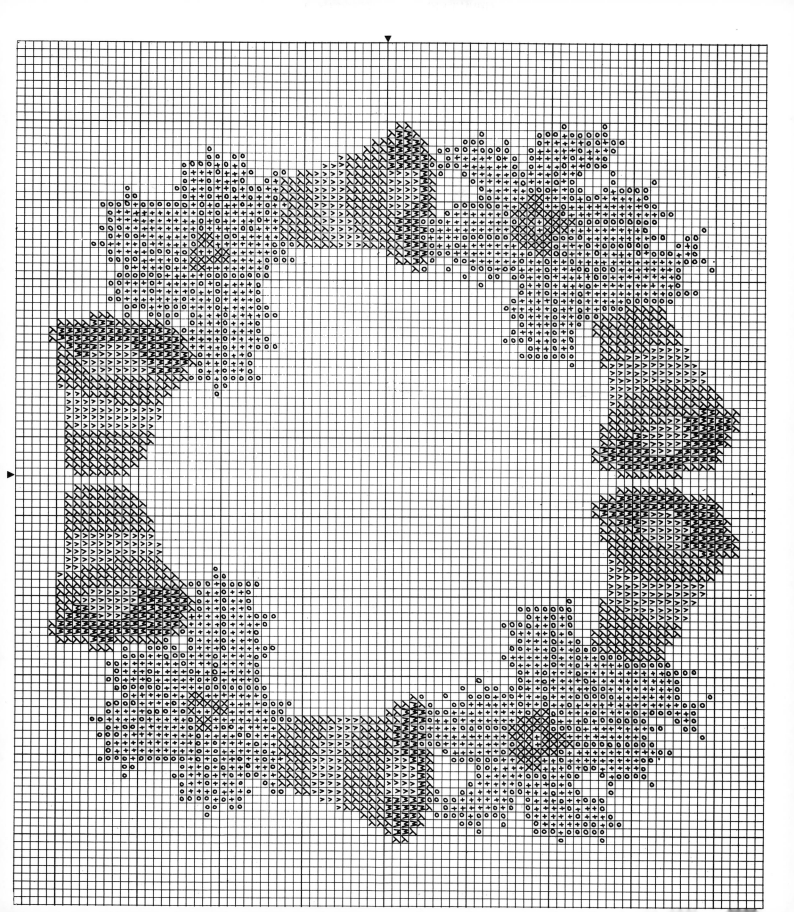

Star of Bethlehem Nativity Scene

Capturing the very essence of Christmas, this project is especially suitable for framing. Joseph leans protectively over Mary and the Christ Child, while the shining star heralds the divine birth.

To form the star, stitch metallic gold thread in half cross stitches over existing stitches; connect the points as shown on the chart. The faces, and one hand, are backstitched in dark grey.

As pictured: Cut size—18½ x 15½". Finished size—14½ x 11½".
#19 even-weave linen; 4 strands of thread.

Y	=	Yellow 444–2 skeins
V	=	Dark Brown 838–1 skein
L	=	Flesh 951–1 skein
●	=	Lavender 718–1 skein
+	=	Magenta 326–1 skein
W	=	White–1 skein
■	=	Metallic Gold Thread–4 yards

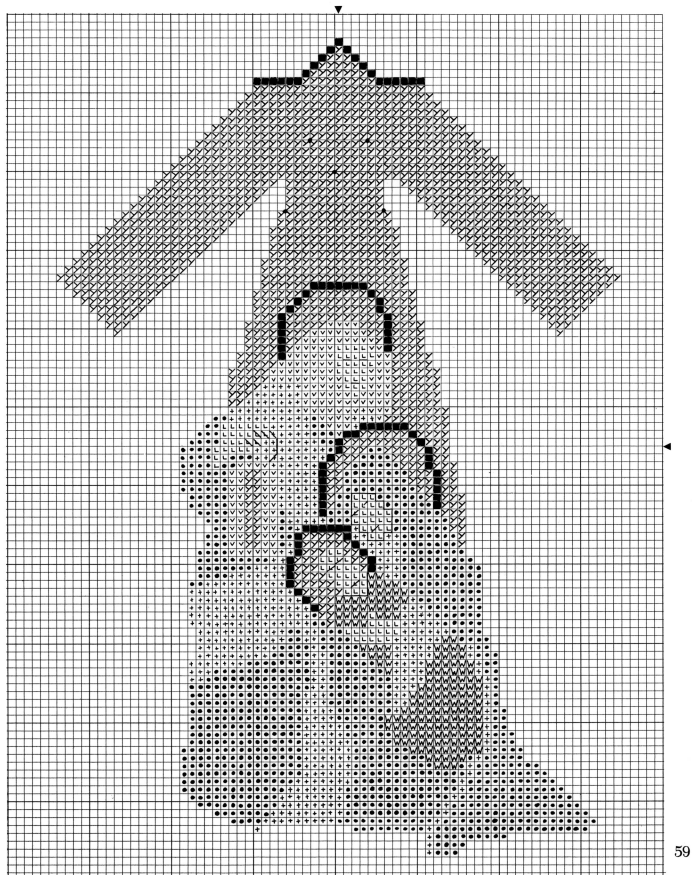

Ornaments of the Season

Here are 18 designs for ornaments that are sure to delight every taste. Leaf through the book, too—there are many figures and separate designs within the other projects that lend themselves very well to being worked as individual ornaments. For example: an elf, angel, flower, leaf, bell, candy cane, gift package, snowflake, bow. Give your imagination full rein and utilize the designs in as many ways as you can think of. (Refer to the color photograph to duplicate the backstitching we did on individual ornaments.)

All of the ornaments pictured here were worked on #14 Aida cotton cloth. The prefabricated, self-adhesive frames shown are easily obtainable in needlecraft stores throughout the country.

1 skein of each color. If you plan to make more than one ornament, it's a good idea to choose colors that can be used in more than one design.

As pictured: Cut size — 5¼″ diameter. Finished size — 3¼″ diameter. #14 Aida cotton cloth; 2 strands of thread.

BUTTERFLY ORNAMENT

% = BLUE 797

● = LIGHT BLUE 799

+ = BROWN 898

V = DARK BEIGE 640

HEART ORNAMENT

% = BLUE 797

X = RED 666

+ = LIGHT GREEN 704

CIRCLED ANGEL ORNAMENT

W = WHITE

+ = DARK BROWN 898

V = FLESH 948

● = BLUE 826

ELF ORNAMENT

Y = YELLOW 973

L = LIGHT GREEN 703

X = RED 666

SQUIRREL ORNAMENT

V = MEDIUM BROWN 400

L = LIGHT GREEN 907

BIRD ORNAMENT

% = BLUE 797

O = GREEN 700

"REJOICE" ORNAMENT

X = RED 666

+ = LIGHT GREEN 704

Y = YELLOW 973

TREE ORNAMENT

/ = DARK GREEN 987

Y = YELLOW 973

V = DARK BROWN 898

BELL ORNAMENT

X = RED 666

V = DARK BROWN 898

+ = LIGHT GREEN 704

/ = DARK GREEN 987

REINDEER ORNAMENT

V = DARK BEIGE 640

GINGER LADY ORNAMENT

+ = DARK BROWN 898

● = LIGHT GREEN 703

CARDINAL ORNAMENT

X = RED 666

B = BLACK

Y = YELLOW 973

V = DARK GOLD 781

CANDLES AND BOW ORNAMENT

X = RED 666

Y = YELLOW 973

‰ = BLUE 797

+ = LIGHT GREEN 704

/ = DARK GREEN 986

CAT ORNAMENT

+ = BROWN 898

V = DARK BEIGE 640

CHURCH ORNAMENT

/ = DARK GREEN 987

W = WHITE

Y = YELLOW 973

+ = DARK BROWN 898

FLOWER ORNAMENT

X = RED 666

Y = YELLOW 973

+ = LIGHT GREEN 704

/ = DARK GREEN 987

ANGEL ORNAMENT

X = RED 666

P = PINK 893

Y = YELLOW 973

C = LIGHT PINK 894

SNOWMAN ORNAMENT

X = RED 666

+ = DARK BROWN 898

W = WHITE

Y = YELLOW 973

Snowflake Pillow

Although no two snowflakes are ever the same, we liked this design so much that we repeated it here as a circle of snow crystals. An attractive reminder of Christmas and wintertime, this simple and appealing pillow will fit into any decor year round—if you like, substitute another color for the blue.

As pictured: Cut size—15½ x 15½″. Finished size—11½ x 11½″.
#19 even-weave linen; 4 strands of thread.

% = Blue 796—4 skeins

■ = Metallic Silver Thread—4 yards

69

"Noel" Saying

With its traditional Christmas message, this saying is an easy project that will brighten your home. You can create another word, initials or greeting—see the Cross Stitch Alphabet on page 137.

As pictured: Cut size—18½ x 13¼". Finished size—14½ x 9¼".
#19 even-weave linen; 4 strands of thread.

● =   Green 700–2 skeins

W =   White–1 skein

X =   Maroon 814–1 skein

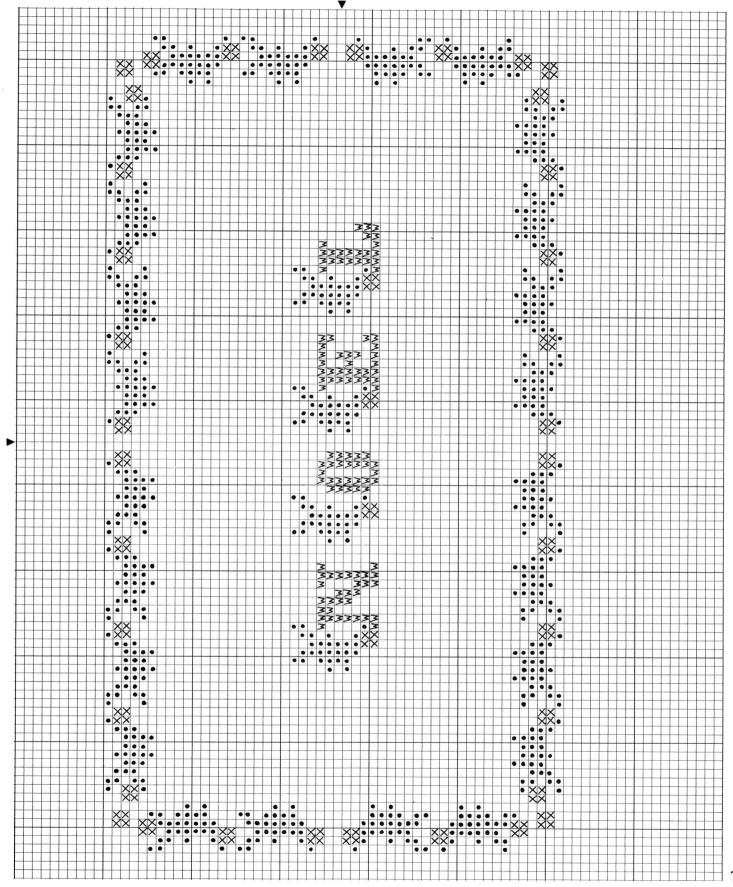

73

Stylized Holiday Motifs

You'll never tire of looking at the intricate patterns worked in this Christmas hanging. (Can you identify the hams? Ham is traditional for Christmas dinner in Sweden.) In fact, you'll probably want to display it all year. It is a time-consuming project that will be both a challenge and a source of great satisfaction for the experienced needleworker.

Note that some figures are repeated, some are mirror-imaged. (See page 6 for tips on mirror-imaging.) Follow both the chart and the photograph closely. Watch the trees—the third, fourth and fifth are mirror-imaged from the first and second. (Work with the photograph here; the spacing will differ when you mirror-image.)

X =   Red 666—8 skeins

As pictured: Cut size — 26 x 19". Finished size — 22 x 15".
#30 even-weave linen; 3 strands of thread.

Pick up repeat here.

Poinsettia Wreath

This colorful wreath includes bells and ornaments along with its splashy bright red poin-settias. It is a mirror-imaged design (see page 6). Instead of making a wreath, you might want to use this pattern for the center of a tablecloth.

As pictured: Cut size—16 x 16″. Finished size—12″ diameter (center is 3¼″ diameter).
#19 even-weave linen; 4 strands of thread.

X = Red 666–2 skeins

B = Black–1 skein

+ = Light Green 704–2 skeins

▲ = Light Orange 972–1 skein

Y = Yellow 973–1 skein

/ = Dark Green 986–1 skein

‰ = Turquoise 996–1 skein

● = Pink 956–1 skein

O = Green 911–1 skein

L = Maroon 902–1 skein

V = Dark Red 321–1 skein

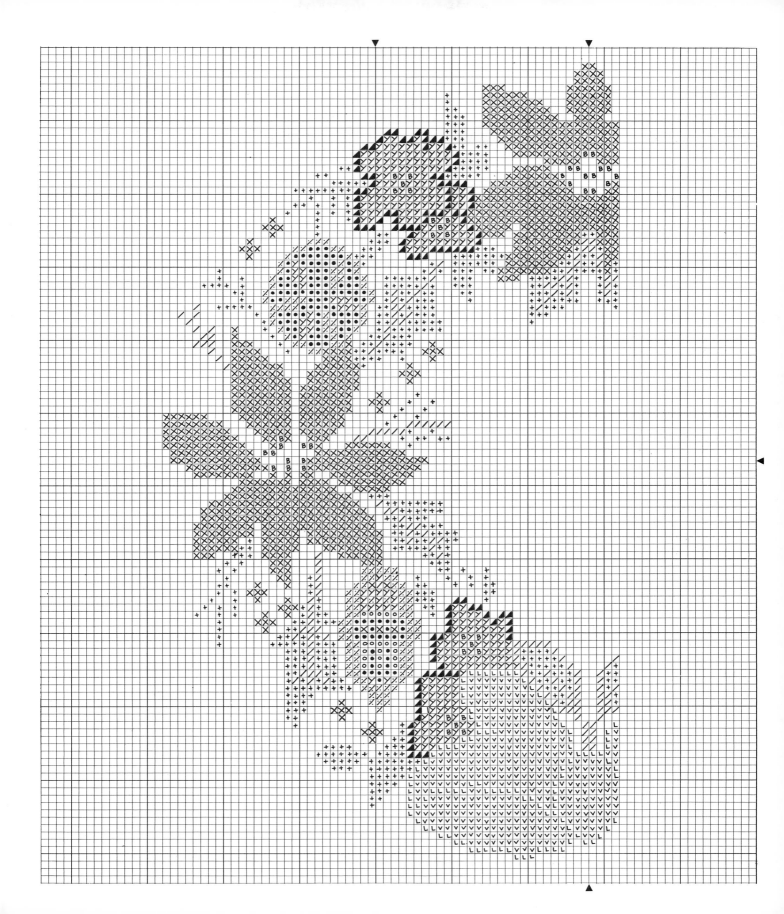

Fruit Basket Runner

The pretty colors of Christmas here are worked in an appealing fruit-and-basket motif. This simple repeat pattern would look equally lovely running down the center of a long tablecloth.

As pictured: Cut size—27¼ x 13½". Finished size—23¼ x 9½".
#19 even-weave linen; 4 strands of thread.

O = Green 700–3 skeins

X = Red 666–3 skeins

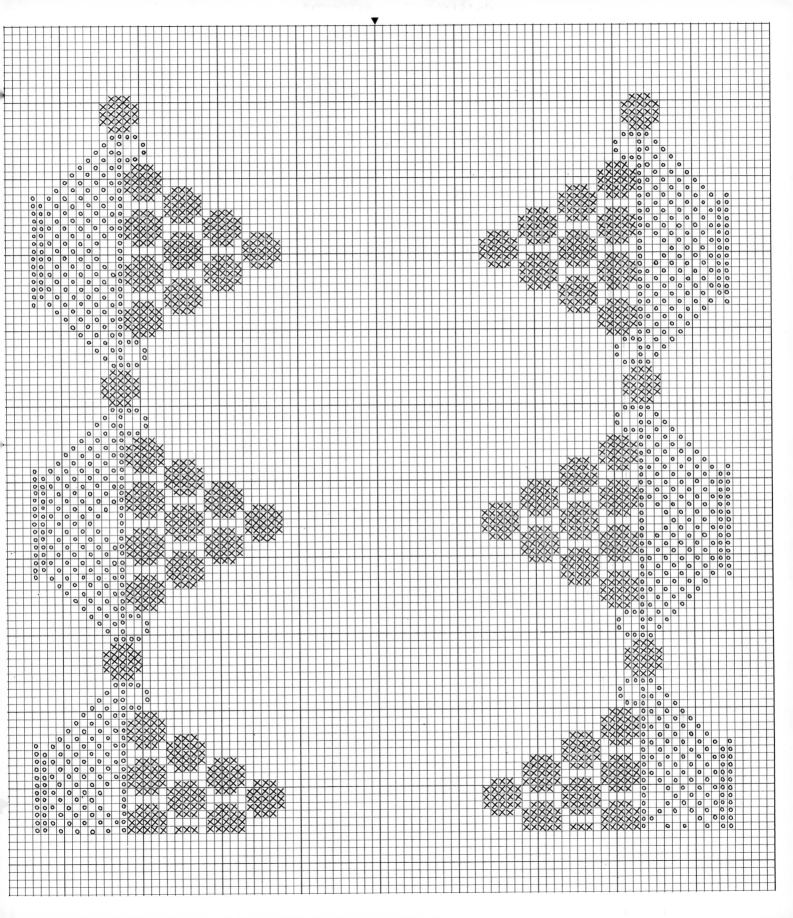

Merry Christmas with Bells On!

A light of happiness and a heart of joy—what a perfect gift! It could also be a warm greeting on your front door. The candle flame is outlined in a metallic gold backstitch.

As pictured: Cut size—15 x 10¾". Finished size—11 x 6¾".
#19 even-weave linen; 4 strands of thread.

X =   Red 666–2 skeins

Y =   Yellow 307–1 skein

O =   Green 700–1 skein

+ =   Grey 414–1 skein

V =   Dark Gold 781–1 skein

■ =   Metallic Gold Thread–4 yards

Heart and Reindeer Place Mat

These two highly stylized designs lend themselves to many treatments. You might repeat them to cover a whole area, forming an overall design that would make a decorative pillow or small hanging. Or each design could be worked individually, and used as an ornament. Each—or both—could also make a pretty border, or center pattern, on a tablecloth.

As pictured: Cut size—15½ x 15½". Finished size—11½ x 11½".
#19 even-weave linen; 4 strands of thread.

X =   Red 304—4 skeins

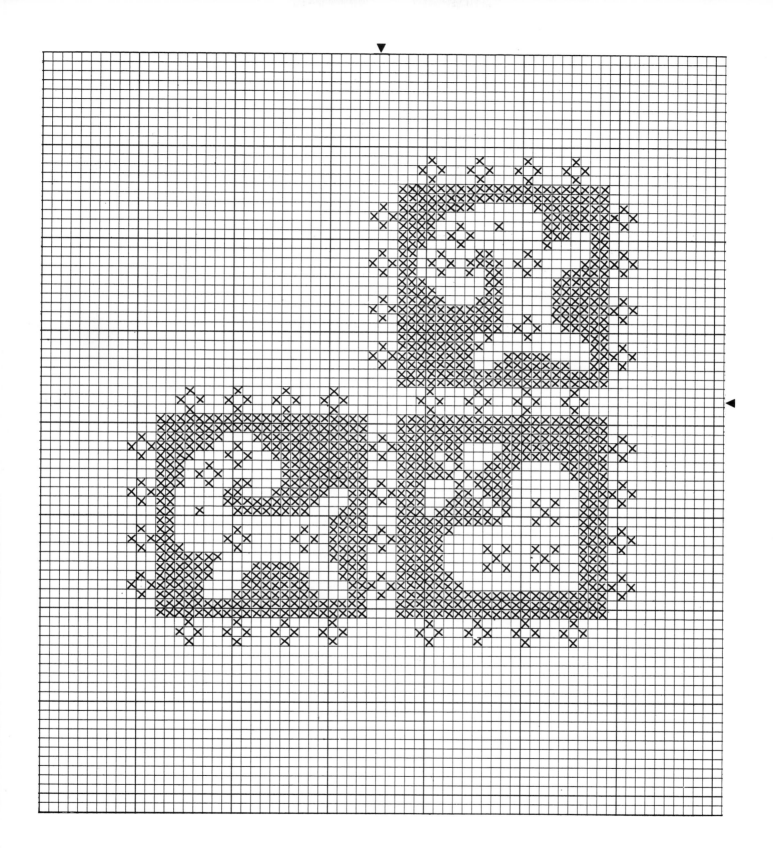

Cat and Santa Christmas Scene

This cat will have tales to tell—he saw Santa! Gazing through a window on a starry night, he almost purrs with holiday contentment. This framed scene is easy to do, and would be especially nice for a child's room. The backstitch is done in black.

As pictured: Cut size—15¾ x 13¾". Finished size—11¾ x 9¾".
#19 even-weave linen; 4 strands of thread.

V = Gold 782–2 skeins

Y = Yellow 726–1 skein

% = Blue 311–1 skein

L = Light Grey 415–1 skein

+ = Dark Grey 317–1 skein

W = White–1 skein

/ = Light Grey 369–1 skein

▼ = Maroon 814–1 skein

◢ = Black–1 skein

X = Red 666–1 skein

O = Green 700–1 skein

● = Flesh 758–1 skein

△ = Dark Beige 840–1 skein

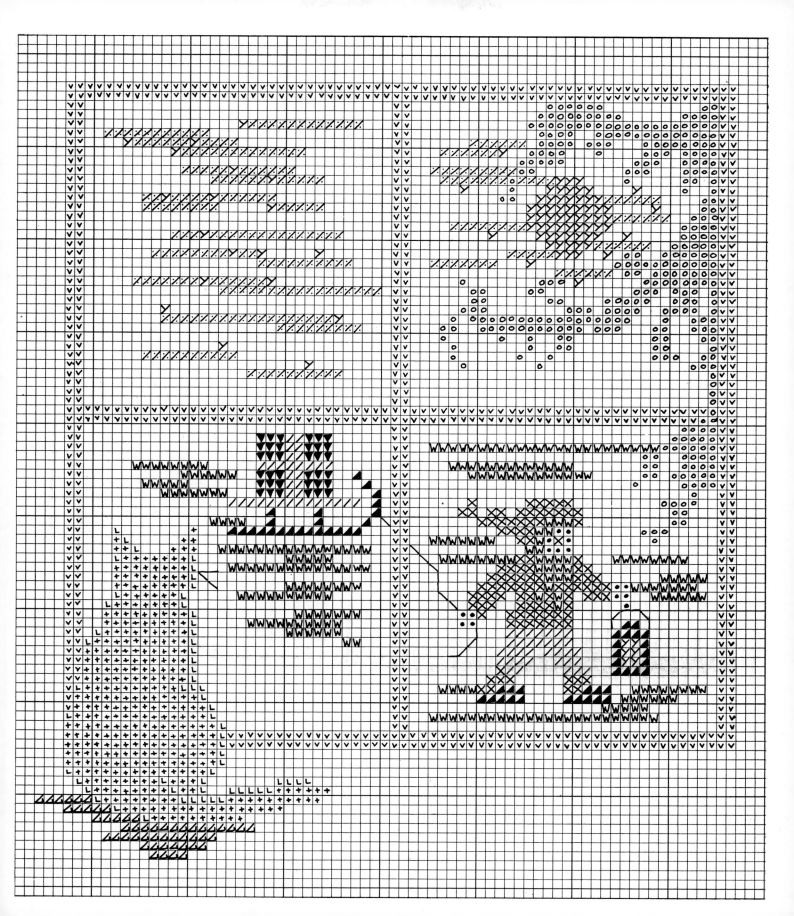

Poinsettia Runner

The vivid poinsettia is very much identified with the gaiety of the Christmas season. The poinsettia motif in this runner is a top to bottom mirror-image. (See page 6 for tips on working with mirror-images.) The middle design on our worked piece (see photograph) is a full repeat. Note that we repeated all but two leaves on both sides of the center. You can also repeat the full design and make the runner as long as you wish. (Note that the chart shows 1½ repeats. The photograph of our worked runner shows one full repeat and two incompletes.) Position the border at the distance desired from the center design.

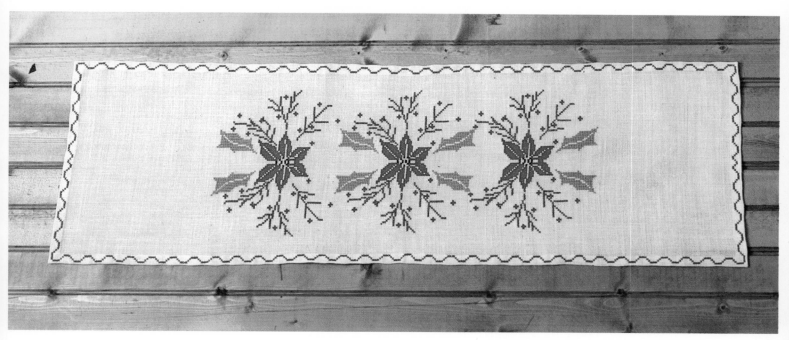

As pictured: Cut size — 45 x 16¾". Finished size — 41 x 12¾".
#19 even-weave linen; 4 strands of thread.

99

X =   Red 666–3 skeins

O =   Green 700–2 skeins

+ =   Light Green 704–2 skeins

B =   Black–1 skein

101

Victorian "Noel"

The elaborately stitched letters form a beautifully designed holiday message. Note that there are three squares, or stitches, in between the "O" and the "E." We've given you a full alphabet of these graceful scripted letters (see the Victorian Alphabet on pages 139-142). Have fun with them, and create your own messages of good will.

As pictured: Cut size—11¼ x 26⅝". Finished size—7¼ x 22⅝".
#19 even-weave linen; 4 strands of thread.

X =   Red 666—3 skeins

103

Candlelight Hand Towels

We worked these on Christmasy red and green backgrounds, using #14 Aida cotton cloth. They'll add a light, happy touch to welcome holiday guests. Place the borders at whatever distance you like from the design.

Y = Yellow 973–2 skeins

W = White–1 skein

+ = Medium Brown 433–1 skein

V = Dark Gold 781–1 skein

● = Maroon 814–1 skein

X = Red 666–1 skein

Y = Yellow 444–2 skeins

W = White–1 skein

O = Green 701–1 skein

+ = Brown 300–1 skein

As pictured: Cut size—17 x 13¼″. Finished size—13 x 9¼″.
#14 Aida cotton cloth; 2 strands of thread.

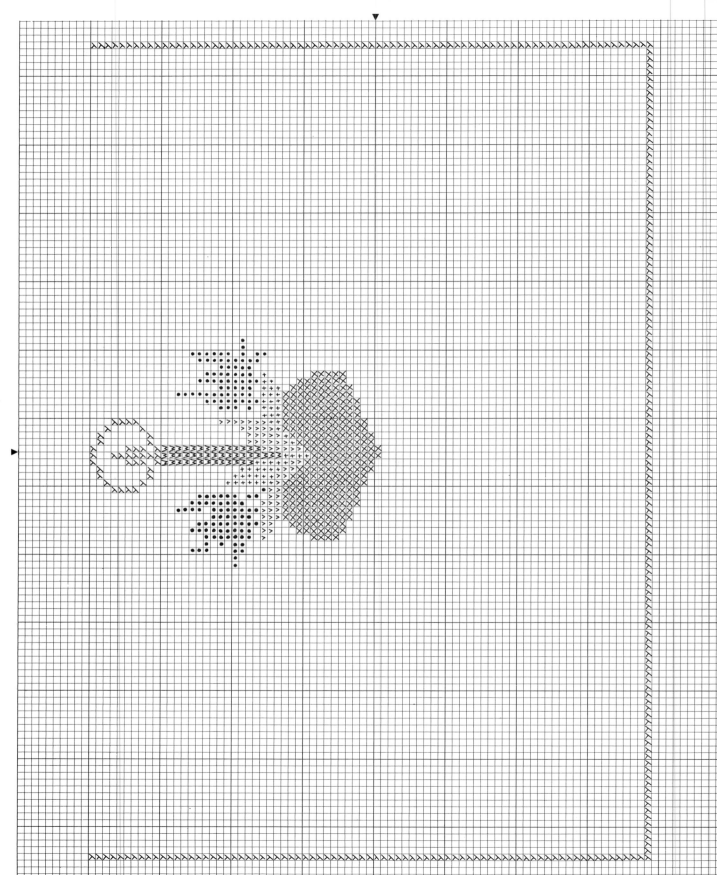

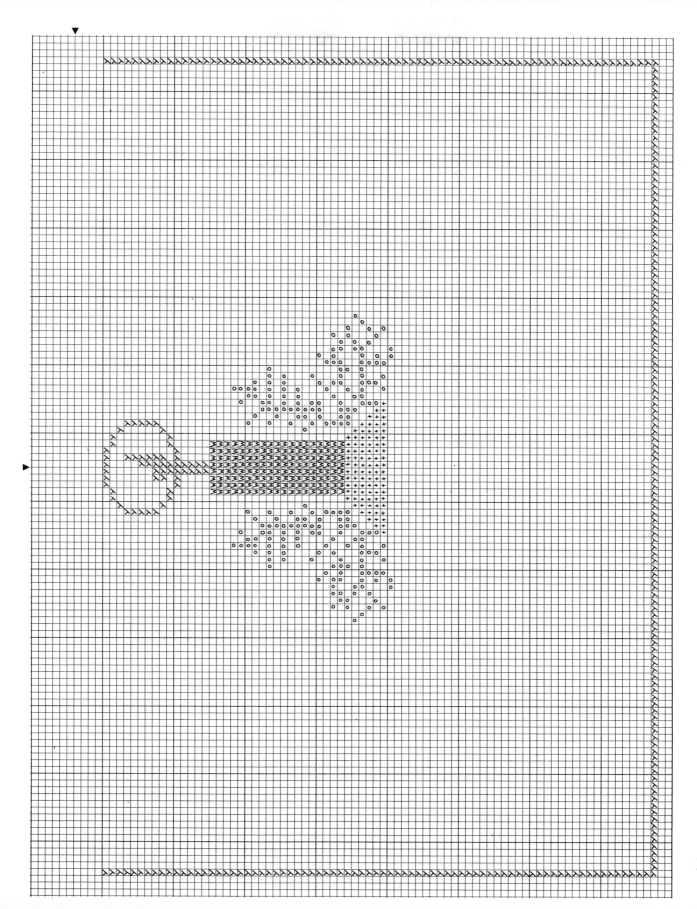

Santa Claus Stocking

Here's a stocking that Santa can't resist filling to the brim! This design is easy and quick to make. Allow extra material if you want to personalize it—maybe for one of your favorite "kids," little or big. (See the Cross Stitch Alphabet on page 137.)

As pictured: Cut size—20 x 14". Finished size—16" long; 8" wide at top.
(These dimensions include enough material for a name.)
#19 even-weave linen; 4 strands of thread.

O = Green 700–2 skeins

W = White–2 skeins

X = Red 666–2 skeins

L = Flesh 948–1 skein

◢ = Dark Grey 317–1 skein

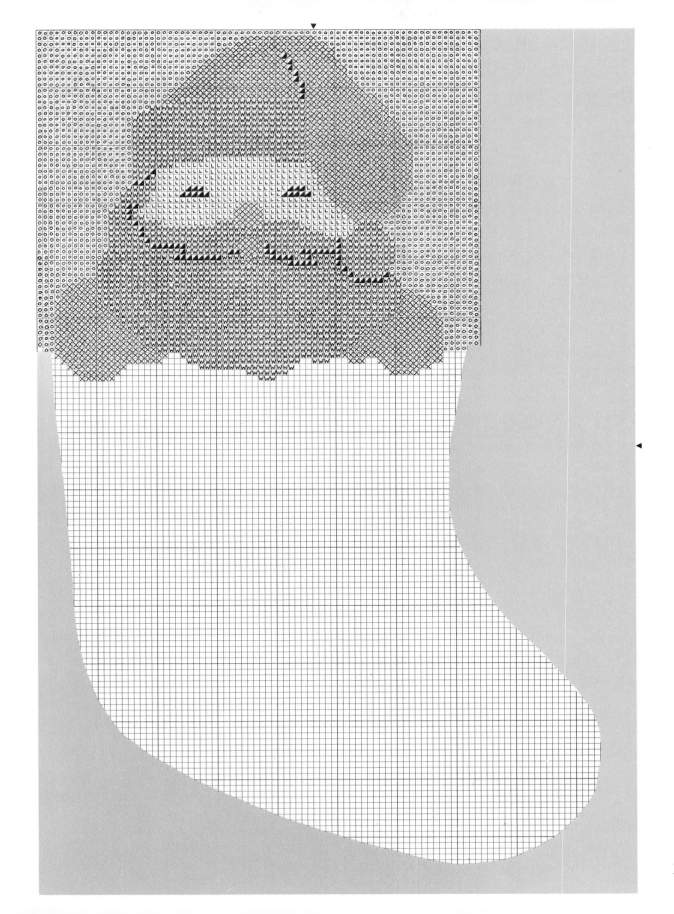

Greens and Berries Wreath

The colors of Christmas brighten this small wreath. Simple but very decorative, it makes a lovely Christmas gift that will in turn welcome guests. It's especially pretty hung on a door or over a fireplace.

As pictured: Cut size—12 x 12". Finished size—8" diameter.
#19 even-weave linen; 4 strands of thread.

O = Green 700–2 skeins

/ = Dark Green 319–2 skeins

◢ = Dark Brown 838–1 skein

X = Red 666–2 skeins

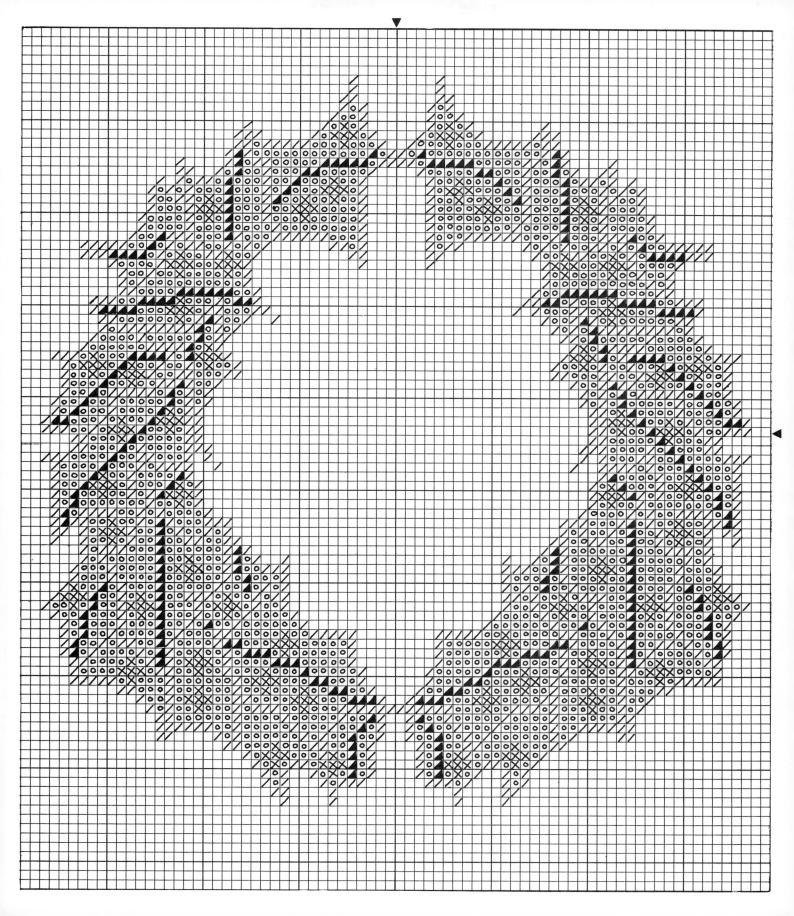

Cabbage Rose Victorian Tray

We incorporated this project into a tray, to show off its beauty. While it's certainly neither easy nor quick to make, it is a very rewarding project, and will give you a great deal of pleasure once it's completed. Take your time with it, and enjoy every stitch. It is of heirloom quality and will be admired and used year round. We left the center open, to accommodate initials or a special saying.

As pictured: Cut size—16 x 12". Finished size—12 x 8".
#30 even-weave linen; 3 strands of thread.

L = Burgundy 902–2 skeins

X = Red 304–2 skeins

● = Dark Pink 3685–2 skeins

P = Medium Pink 3687–2 skeins

C = Light Pink 3689–2 skeins

/ = Dark Green 890–2 skeins

O = Medium Green 3347–2 skeins

+ = Light Green 471–2 skeins

V = Dark Olive Green 367–2 skeins

T = Light Olive Green 368–2 skeins

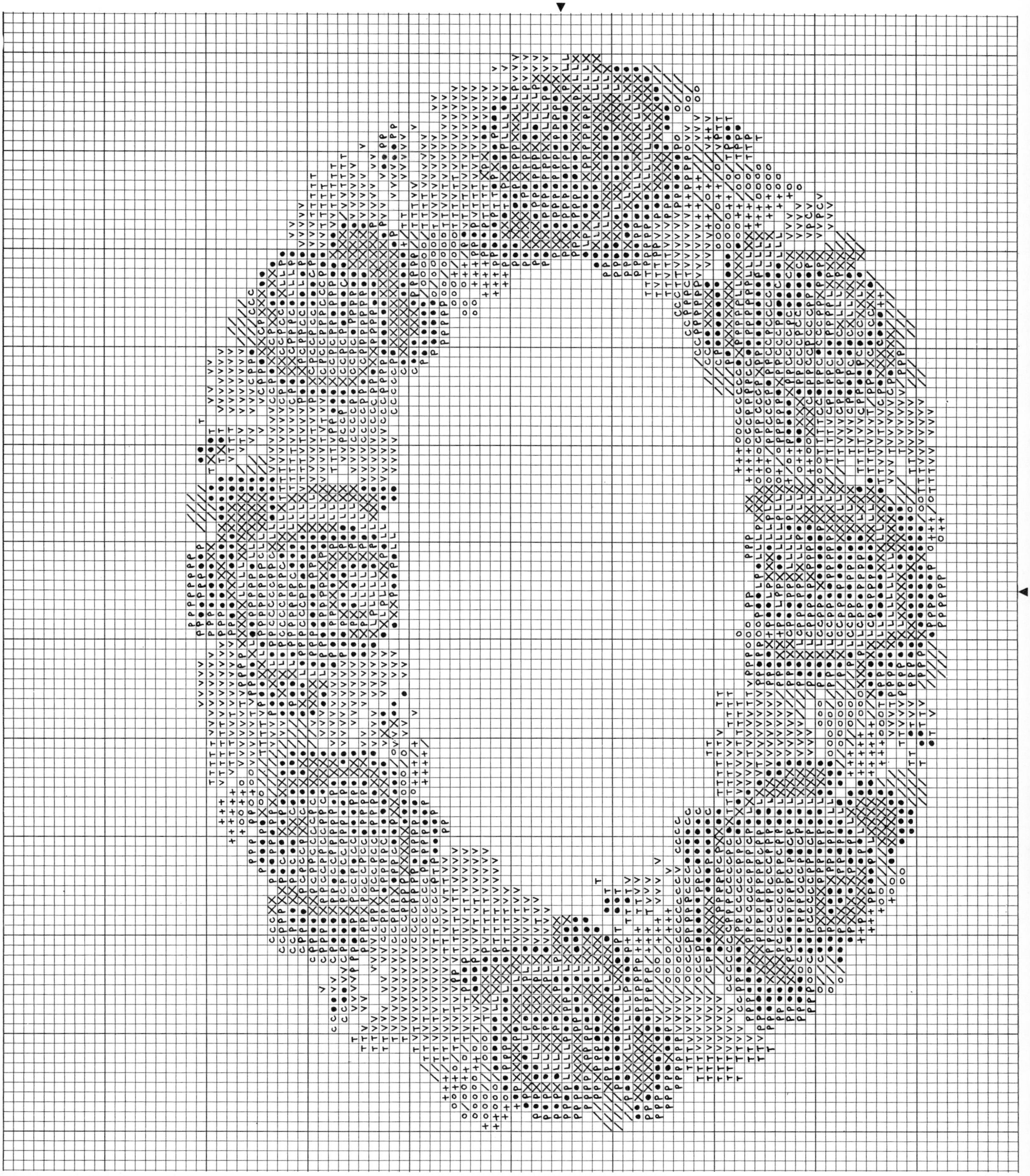

"Joy to the World" Saying

A message that makes an irresistible gift, emphasizing what Christmas is all about. The flourish of bows makes a nice frame to set it off. We outlined the bows and bottom part of the branches in a green backstitch.

As pictured: Cut size—18½ x 13¼". Finished size—14½ x 9¼".
#19 even-weave linen; 4 strands of thread.

X = Maroon 815–1 skein

● = Light Green 703–1 skein

W = White–1 skein

Santa's Pack Card Holder

Santa is loaded down with goodies, and this card holder is meant to be filled with Christmas cards from family and friends. Share the enjoyment with one and all by gathering the greetings into this attention-getting display.

You can replace the horn with your initials or name, if you like (see the Cross Stitch Alphabet on page 137). Santa's beard is outlined in a dark grey backstitch. When you stitch the pouch, be sure to fold the material up toward Santa. Because you are working with one piece of material, uncut, you will stitch the pouch as it faces you. In other words, you'll stitch it on the side opposite the side you've cross stitched.

X = Red 666–2 skeins

% = Blue 820–1 skein

W = White–1 skein

V = Dark Gold 781–1 skein

O = Green 910–1 skein

Y = Yellow 726–1 skein

L = Flesh 948–1 skein

◢ = Dark Grey 317–1 skein

As pictured: Cut size — 20 x 12½". Finished size — 16 x 8½". (Length includes pocket, which is 5⅝" deep.)
#19 even-weave linen; 4 strands of thread.

Merry Christmas, World!

This long hanging (see next 4 pages) is a favorite project, truly of heirloom quality. Although it isn't easy, it certainly is worth the time and skill entailed, for it's one of the most beautiful and elegant pieces in the book.

Hung from a wall or your front door, it will proclaim a warm welcome and season's greeting to all who come to your home. It has a variety of wonderful Christmas motifs— for example, the circles represent a very decorative holiday bread that is traditional in Sweden. It can be worked in sections if you wish—an individual portion would make a stunning smaller hanging or "picture" to be framed.

X =   Red 666—8 skeins

■ =   Metallic Gold Thread—4 yards

128　　**As pictured:** Cut size — 41½ x 15½". Finished size — 37½ x 11½".
#30 even-weave linen; 3 strands of thread.

Pick up repeat here.

Pick up repeat here.

Christmas Calendar

Father Christmas himself—as real as life—in a gorgeous Christmas calendar! Wouldn't we all love to have this, to heighten the anticipation before the big day? A small parcel for each of the 24 days before Christmas can be hung from each ring. We placed the days at random, just to add to the fun. The white stitches at Santa's feet are mixed with grey (we used two strands of each color). Highlight Santa's beard in grey backstitches, placed as you wish. (You can follow what we did by looking at the photograph, but we do encourage you to give him your own touch.) We outlined his eyes in a medium blue backstitch.

This calendar is an elaborate and time-consuming project, but well worth the effort—it will bring joy and smiles for many years to come.

/ = Dark Green 986—4 skeins

X = Red 304—4 skeins

● = Gold 782—2 skeins

L = Dark Grey 317—1 skein

V = Brown 898—2 skeins

W = White—2 skeins

+ = Light Green 368—2 skeins

◢ = Flesh 948—1 skein

% = Medium Blue 793—1 skein

As pictured: Cut size—26½ x 20". Finished size—22½ x 16".
#19 even-weave linen; 4 strands of thread.

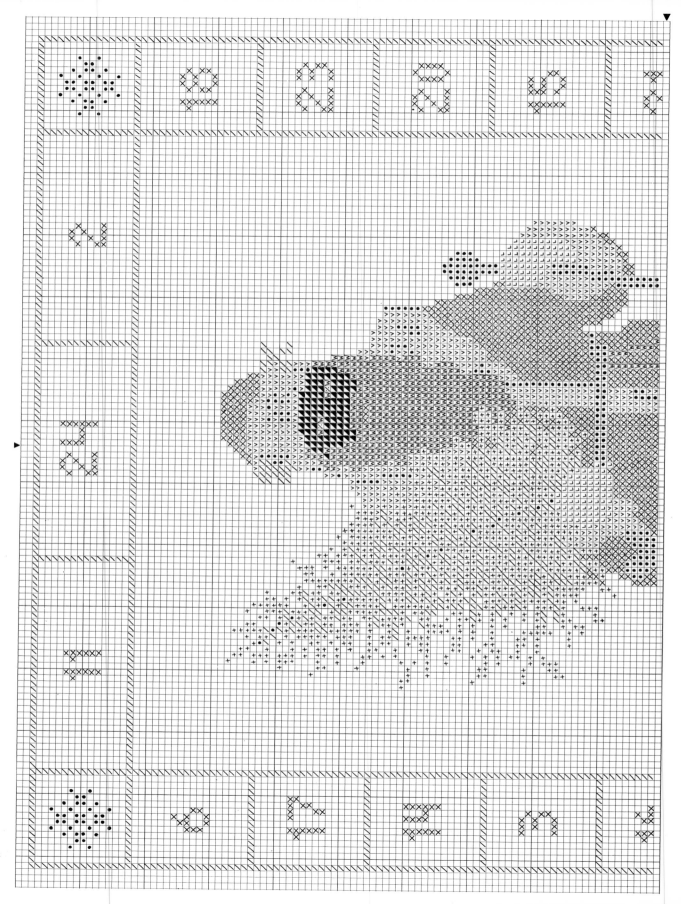

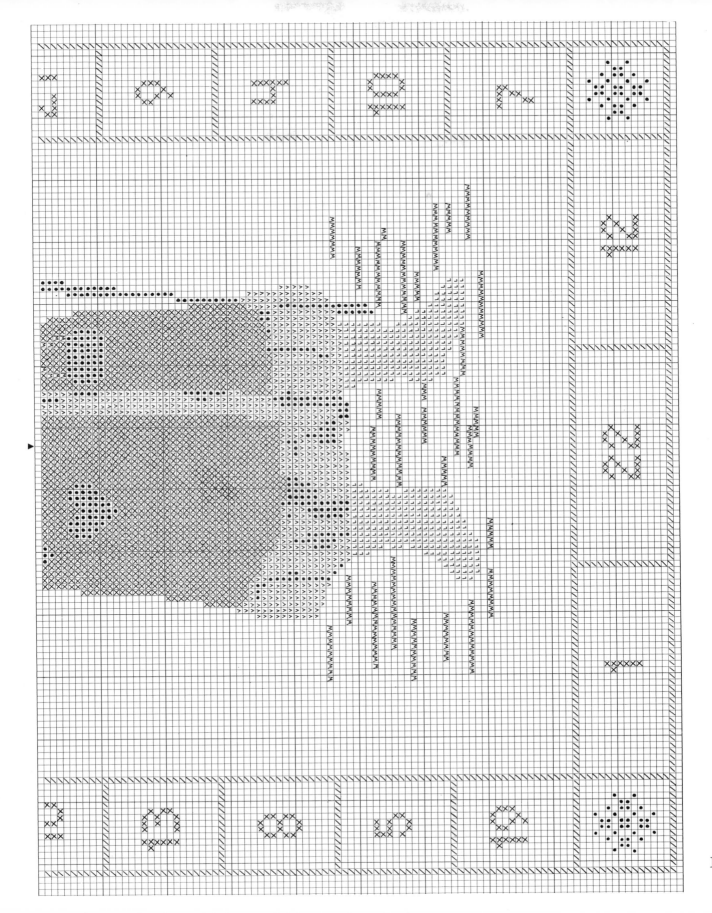

135

Cross Stitch Alphabet

Cross Stitch Numbers

For Alphabet:

W = White

● = Green 700

X = Maroon 814

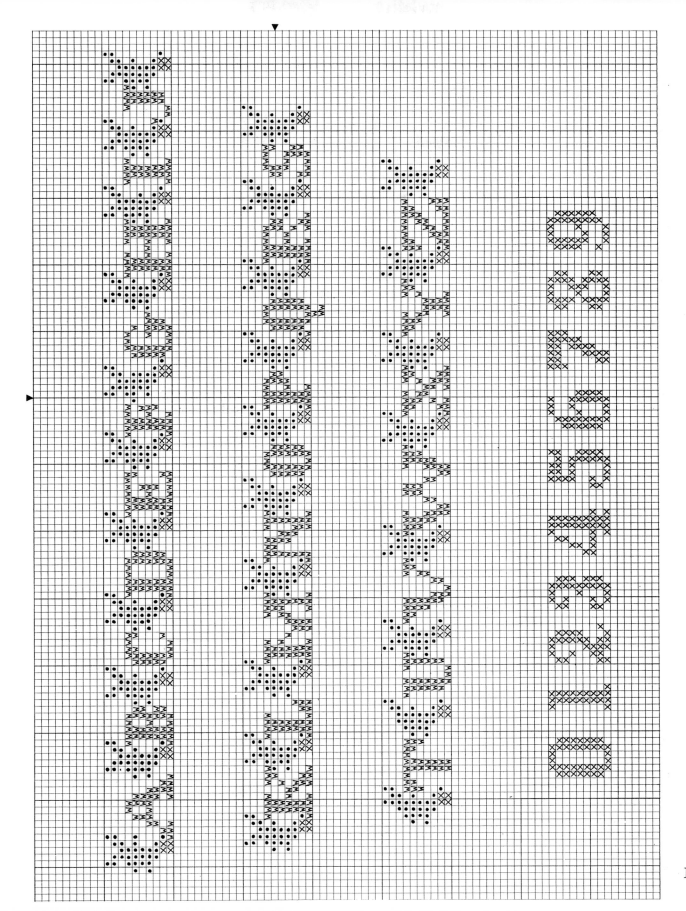

Cross Stitch Victorian Alphabet

139

140

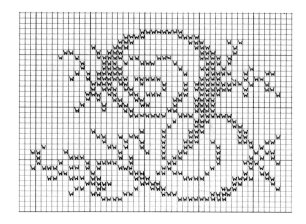

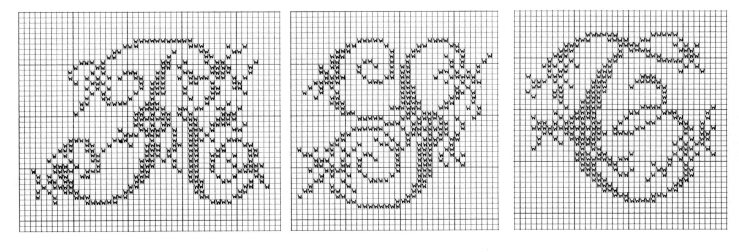

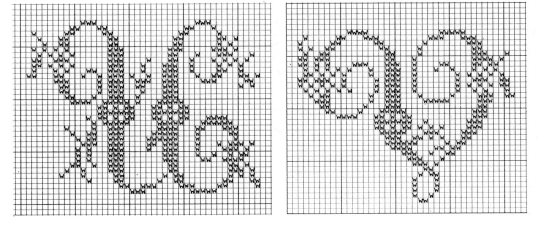

141

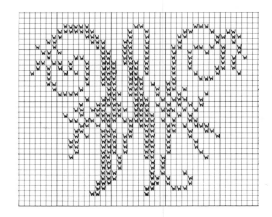

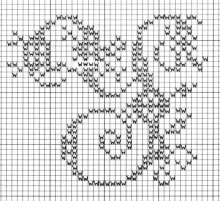

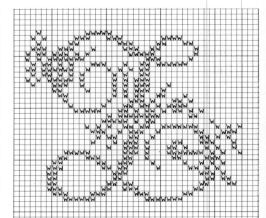

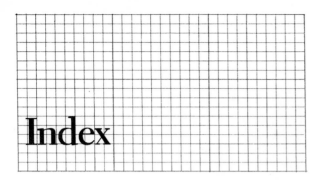

Index

Make
your home
special

Since 1922, millions of men and women have turned to *Better Homes and Gardens* magazine for help in making their homes more enjoyable places to be. You, too, can trust *Better Homes and Gardens* to provide you with the best in ideas, inspiration and information for better family living.

In every issue you'll find ideas on food and recipes, decorating and furnishings, crafts and hobbies, remodeling and building, gardening and outdoor living plus family money management, health, education, pets, car maintenance and more.

For information on how you can have *Better Homes and Gardens* delivered to your door, write to: Mr. Robert Austin, P.O. Box 4536, Des Moines, IA 50336.

Better Homes and Gardens ®

*The Idea Magazine
for Better Homes
and Families*

144